My First
Recorder
Book

By Janet Bunting

Collins

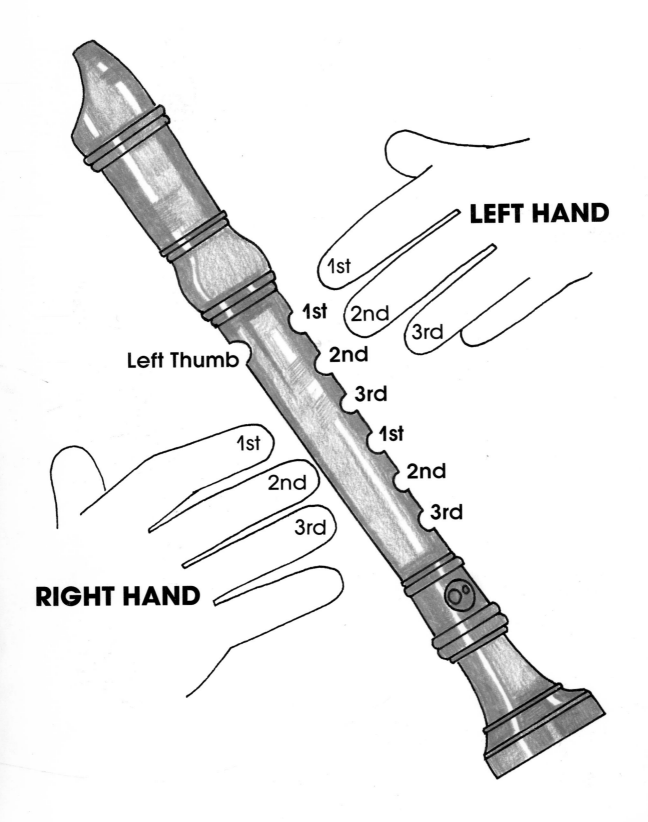

LEFT HAND

1st

1st

2nd

2nd

3rd

3rd

Left Thumb

1st

2nd

3rd

1st

2nd

3rd

RIGHT HAND

How to hold your recorder

Hold your recorder in front of you with both hands, the left hand at the top.

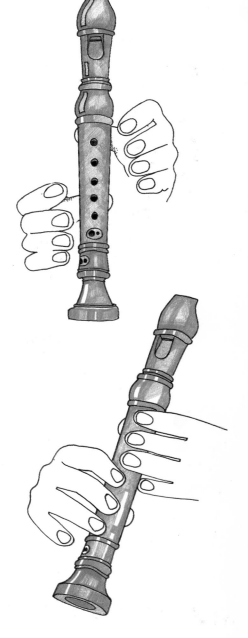

Place the first three fingers of your left hand on the first three holes. Cover the hole underneath with your left thumb.

Now put the first three fingers of your right hand over the 3 lower holes. Your right thumb should support the recorder underneath.

Look at the picture to see if you are holding the recorder correctly.

Use the pads of your fingers and not the tips to cover the holes. Press down firmly but not too hard.

Remember, left hand at the top.

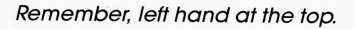

A bit about music

Musical notes are written on lines called a *stave.* There are 5 lines in a stave.

The higher the notes go on the stave, the higher the sound is!

The sign at the beginning is called a *treble clef*.

Notes on the stave are separated by lines.

These are called *bar lines* and the space between these bar lines is called a *bar.*

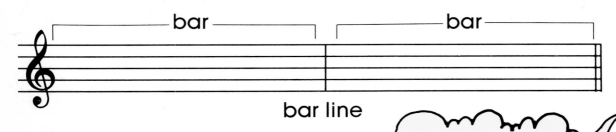

bar   bar

bar line

We are now ready to learn to play our first note.

A double bar line means that the music is all finished.

4

Note B

The note **B** sits on the third line of the stave.

To play the note **B**, lift up most of your fingers except the first finger of your left hand and your left thumb.

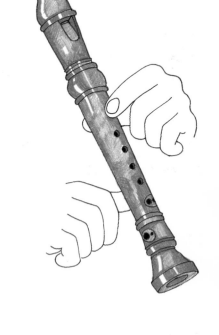

Your right hand thumb can stay where it is, supporting the recorder. All other fingers should be away from the holes.

Hold your recorder up to your mouth and place your lips over the mouthpiece. Don't let your teeth touch the mouthpiece.

Blow very gently into the recorder. Make your tongue say the word *'du'* while you are blowing.

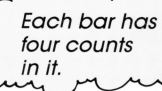

Each bar has four counts in it.

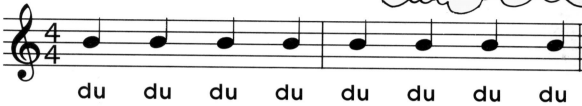

du   du   du   du   du   du   du   du

Play this note several times. Try to make each note sound the same length.

5

Your first tune

Look at the music below. Say the words to the song. Now clap in time with the words as you say them.

Do this several times until you know the words without looking.

Using the note **B**, play the tune on the recorder.

Blow one note **B** for each note of music, singing the words of the song in your mind.

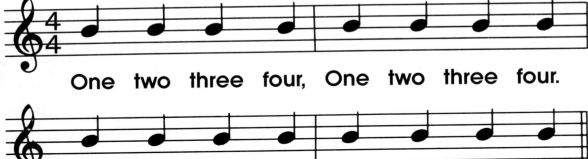

One two three four, One two three four.

Tam – my's wait – ing   by   the front door.

Practice it several times until you can make really clear notes.

Don't forget - only your first finger and thumb of your left hand should cover the holes.

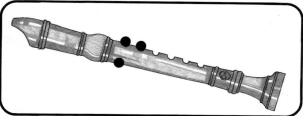
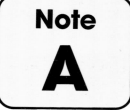

Notice how note **A** is sitting in the space between the second and third lines of the stave.

Whenever you see a note in this position on the stave you will know that this is note **A**.

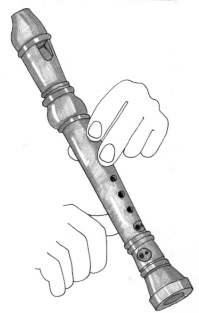

To play note **A** put your fingers in the same position as for note **B** and then put the second finger of your left hand on the second hole.

Look at the picture, are your fingers in the same position?

Each bar has four counts in it.

Play the note **A** several times. Remember to blow gently.

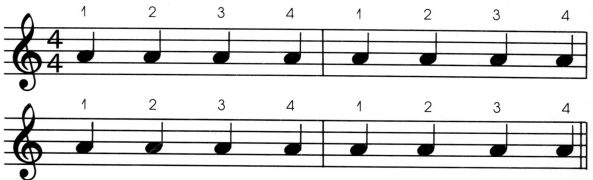

Note Values

The notes you have been
playing are called *crotchets*.
Notice how it has a black body
and a long stem. A crotchet is
worth 1 count.

This note is called a *minim*.
It has a white body and a long
stem. A minim is worth 2 counts.
You have to play a minim for
twice as long as a crotchet.

These notes are called *quavers*.
Quavers look like crotchets but
have a little tail on the stem.
1 quaver is worth half a count.
2 quavers joined together are
worth 1 count.

Say the words of the song.
Then using note **A**, play the notes.
Blow one note for each crotchet,
two short notes for the quavers
and one long note for each minim.

It helps to say "and" after each count when you are playing quavers.

Tam – my finds her new note A,

She is hap – py learn –ing to play.

This is a dotted minim and is worth 3 counts.

A dot after any note makes the note half as long again.

Every line in this next tune ends with a dotted minim - be sure to hold it for 3 counts. Clap and say-sing the words first.

Three counts here.

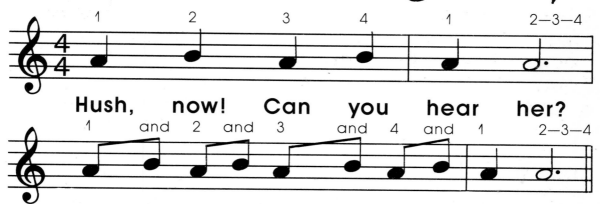

Hush, now! Can you hear her?

Tam – my cat is play – ing the re – cor – der.

Now you are ready to try some tunes using notes **B** and **A** in the same song.

Put your fingers in the position for note **A**.

Blow gently for note **A**.
While you are still blowing,
lift the second finger of the
left hand away from the hole.
You are now playing the note **B**.

Take a breath and repeat this several times so that you can play note **A** and note **B** just by lifting one finger away from the hole.

Say the words of the song first.
Then count each note. 1 count for a crotchet, half a count for each quaver and 2 counts for the minim.

Now see if you can play the music on your recorder.

Say it, then clap it.

Oth – er cats are rea – lly a – mazed at
eve – ry note that Tam – my plays.

10

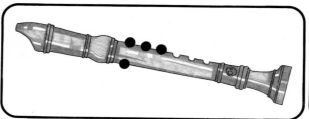

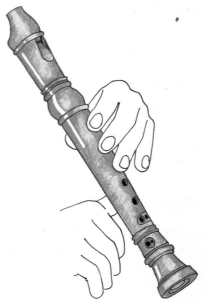

The note **G** sits on the second line of the stave.

To play the note **G** put your fingers in position for note **A**. Now add the third finger of the left hand over the third hole. This is note **G**.

Practice this exercise several times before you go on.

Good−ness, gra-cious! Now I'm play – ing G.

Play note **G**, then lift the third finger and play note **A**, now lift the second finger and play note **B**.

Now comes the hard part! After playing note **B**, you have to put both the second and third fingers back on their holes at the same time.

Can you recognise the beginning of this well-known tune?

Tunes to play

Tam – my's bus – y as a bum – ble bee,

Prac – tic – ing so care – ful – ly.

Tam-my's hav-ing trou-ble with her fur-ry lit-tle paws,

She wish-es she had nim-ble fing-ers just like yours.

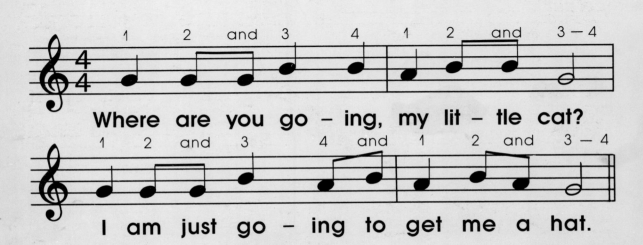

Where are you go – ing, my lit – tle cat?

I am just go – ing to get me a hat.

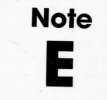

Note **E** is easy to recognise as it sits on the first line of the stave.

To play note **E**, first put your fingers in position for note **G**. Now add the first and second fingers of the right hand.

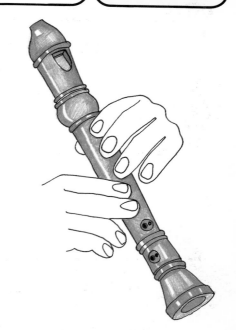

Make sure your right thumb is supporting your recorder.

Practice note **E** on its own and then try this tune.

Lower notes such as note **E** need to be blown very gently.

13

Time signature

At the beginning of every tune there are 2 numbers. The top number tells you how many counts in each bar of music.

These numbers are called a *time signature*.

If it says 4, then there are 4 counts in every bar.

In the next piece of music there will be 2 counts in every bar.

Clap the counts first. 2 counts for a minim, half a count for the quavers and 1 count for the crotchets.

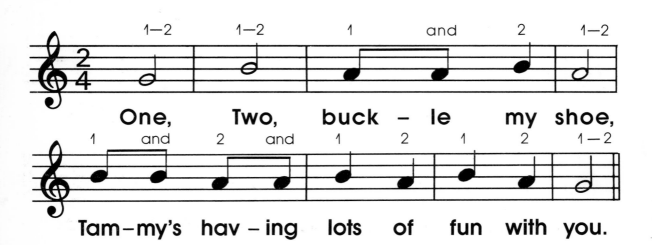

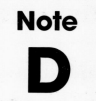
The note **D** sits just below the first line.

First play the note **E**. Now add the third finger of your right hand. There are two little holes to cover for note **D**.

Hold your recorder correctly and cover the holes carefully so that there are no squeaks.

You are now using 3 fingers of each hand and your left thumb.

Clap the counts first.

Remember that lower notes need less air if they are to sound clear.

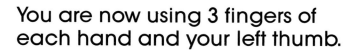

D   is   such   a   qui – et   note,

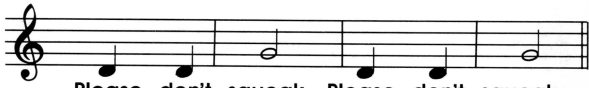

Please don't squeak. Please don't squeak.

The crotchet rest

This sign tells you to rest for 1 count. When you see a crotchet rest, wait 1 count before playing the next note.

Count and clap these little tunes. Now practice playing each line.

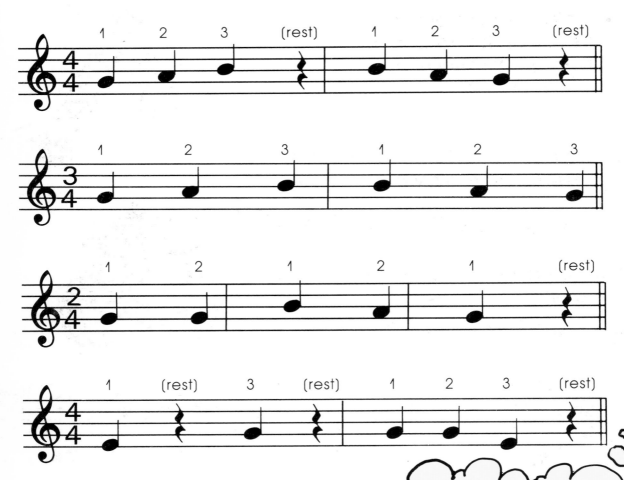

Remember to check the top number at the beginning of each tune so that you know how many counts there are in a bar.

You can say "rest" to yourself each time you see a crotchet rest.

This is note **C**. Notice how it is sitting in the space between the third and fourth lines of the stave.

To play note **C** put your fingers in position for note **A**. Now lift up the first finger of your left hand.

Practice note **C** several times on its own before playing this tune.

Remember to blow gently all the time.

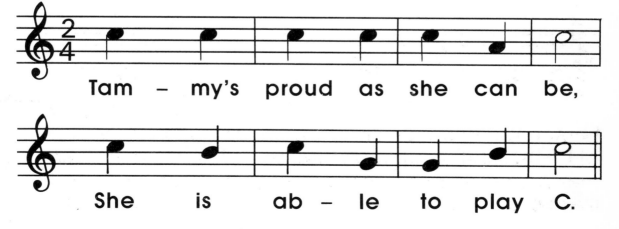

Tam – my's proud as she can be,

She is ab – le to play C.

The repeat sign :||

This sign tells you to repeat the tune.

You go back to the beginning and play the tune again.

Although you can only see 2 lines of music for this tune, there are 4 lines of words. At the end of the last bar you will see the repeat sign.

Play the music once for the first line of words and then play the music again for the second verse.

This tune uses notes **B**, **A** and **G**.

You stop after the second time - don't go on playing forever!

| La – zy | Tam – my's | by | the | fire, |
| Tam – my | come | and | play | with | me |

Wake up Tam – my don't you tire.
If you want to earn your tea.

18

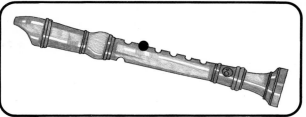

High D

High **D** is found on the 4th line of the stave.

To play high **D**, first play **C** and then move your left thumb away from the hole underneath.
Your right thumb should continue to support your recorder.

Remember, blow gently and make sure your fingers are firmly over each hole. If any note squeaks, you are probably not covering the holes properly.

Clap it, then play it.

Practice this exercise several times before you go on.

We have learned to play high D,

Tam – my's play – ing mer – ri – ly.

The tie

A tie joins together two notes that sound the same.

Do not play the second note but join both notes together to make one long sound.

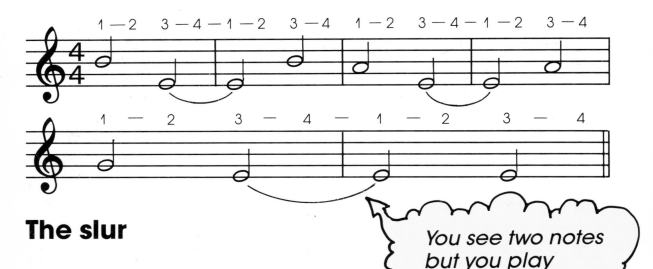

The slur

A slur looks like a tie but this time the notes are different.

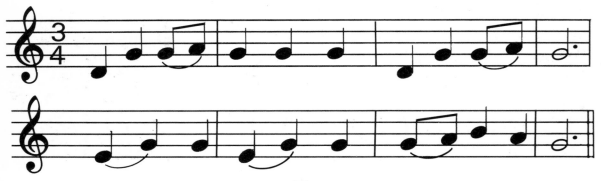

You see two notes but you play only one.

The curved line means the two notes should not be separated. Play the first note and then change fingers but don't take a breath or say *'du'* in between. Keep blowing through the second note.

The note **F#** is found in the space between the first and second lines of the stave.

To play note **F#**, put your fingers in the position for note **G** and add the second and third fingers of your right hand.

Practice **F#** on its own first.

Now try to play this tune.

Tam – my   has   to   use   her   tail   to

get   to   F   sharp   on   the   scale.

You don't usually write a sharp sign before each **F** on the stave. Instead, you will see this sign on the **F** line at the beginning of the music.

When you see this sign, every **F** in the music will be an **F#**.

You have now learned eight notes.

As the notes go up the stave, the sound gets higher.

This is how they all look together on the stave.

D   E   F♯   G   A   B   C   D'

This tune uses all eight notes, clap, count and sing first, then play the tune.

Play slowly at first, then build up speed.

Tom he was a pi – per's son, He

learned to play when he was young, But

all the tune that he could play was

"O – ver the hills and far a – way."

Play it several times.

The semibreve

This is a *semibreve*.

A semibreve has a white body but no tail. This note is worth 4 counts.

1 semibreve will fill a 4/4 bar. Play these semibreves taking care to breathe gently and evenly for the 4 counts.

Use the numbers above the bars to help you count this tune. Clap and count it before playing.

Can you see the line with the repeat sign? Don't forget to play this line twice.

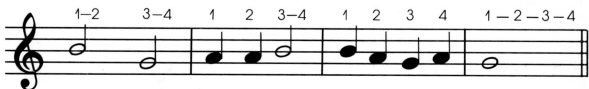

Starting with part of a bar

Sometimes a piece of music starts on the last count of the bar, but the missing counts are found at the end of the music.
This is called an *anacrusis*.

See if you can recognise the beginnings of these tunes, which all start on the last count of the bar.

Count 1 2 3 - start on count 4.

Count 1 2 - start on count 3.

Count 1 2 - start on count 3.

Playing staccato notes

A dot under or over a note tells
you to play the note staccato.
This means you must make the note
short. This is like short hops between
each dotted note.

Try saing *'dut'* instead of
'du' as you blow.

dut   dut   dut   dut   dut   dut   dut   dut

Now repeat these notes playing
them normally, or smoothly.
Can you hear the difference?
Both versions should be played
at the same speed.

The next tune uses both smooth
and staccato notes.

dut dut dut dut dut dut dut dut du-u du-u du du

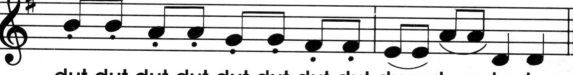

dut dut dut dut dut dut dut dut du-u du-u du du

More tunes to play

You are now ready to try some tunes using the notes you have learned.

Count and clap them and say – sing the words first.

Then see if you can play the music on your recorder.

The Grand Old Duke of York

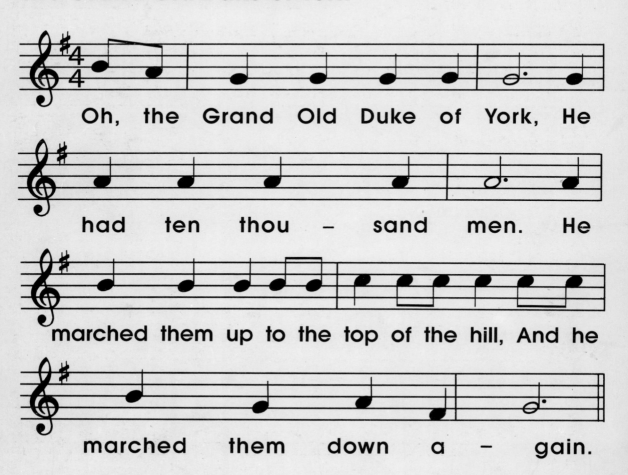

Oh, the Grand Old Duke of York, He had ten thou – sand men. He marched them up to the top of the hill, And he marched them down a – gain.

One Man Went to Mow

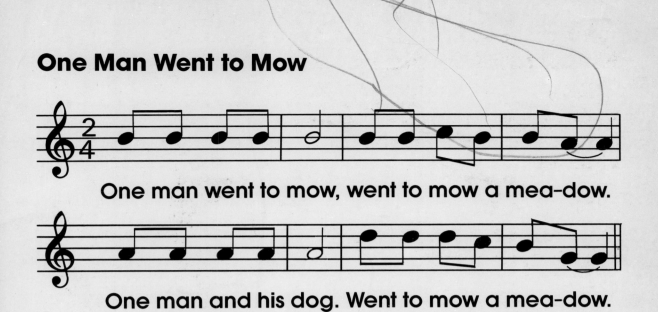

One man went to mow, went to mow a mea-dow.

One man and his dog. Went to mow a mea-dow.

There's a Hole in My Bucket

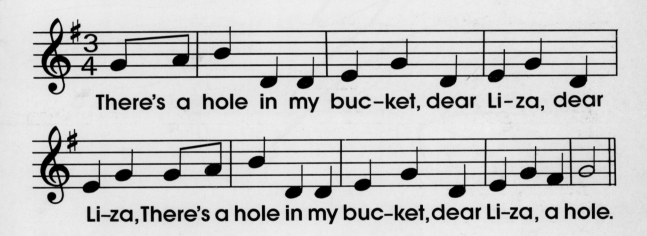

There's a hole in my buc-ket, dear Li-za, dear

Li-za, There's a hole in my buc-ket, dear Li-za, a hole.

Ode to Joy

Beethoven

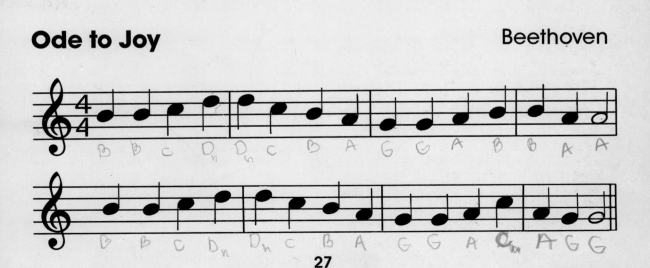

Hot Cross Buns

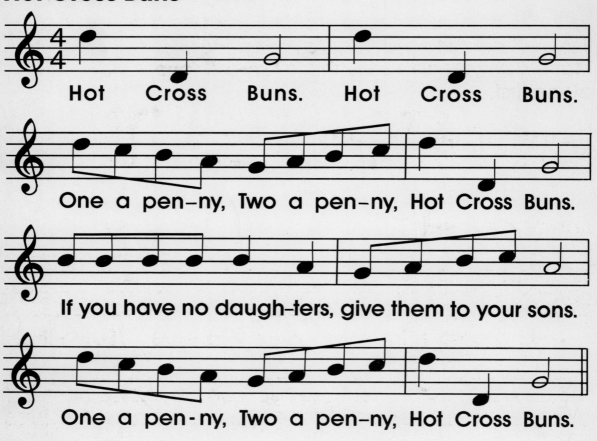

Hot   Cross   Buns.   Hot   Cross   Buns.

One a pen-ny, Two a pen-ny, Hot Cross Buns.

If you have no daugh-ters, give them to your sons.

One a pen-ny, Two a pen-ny, Hot Cross Buns.

Amazing Grace

A-ma-zing grace, how sweet the sound, that

saved a wretch like me. I once was lost but now am

found,   was   blind   but   now   can   see.

Some rounds to play

It is a lot of fun to play music with a friend.
Make sure you can play these tunes comfortably
alone first.

Then one player starts at the beginning and
the second player joins in when the first reaches **2**.

London's Burning

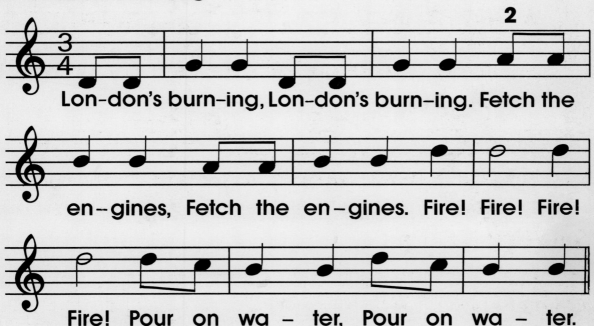

Lon-don's burn-ing, Lon-don's burn-ing. Fetch the

en--gines, Fetch the en-gines. Fire! Fire! Fire!

Fire! Pour on wa – ter, Pour on wa – ter.

Canon by Thomas Tallis

Notes for parents

Note values

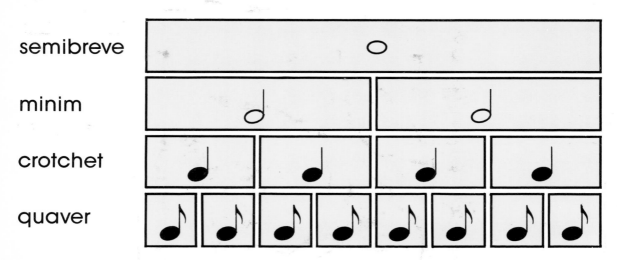

semibreve	
minim	
crotchet	
quaver	

A dot after a note lengthens its sound by half its value.

Time signatures

2 crotchet counts in a bar

3 crotchet counts in a bar

4 crotchet counts in a bar

Sharps

A sharp raises a note by one semitone. When a sharp sign follows the treble clef, this is called the key signature.

Fingering chart for notes used in this book

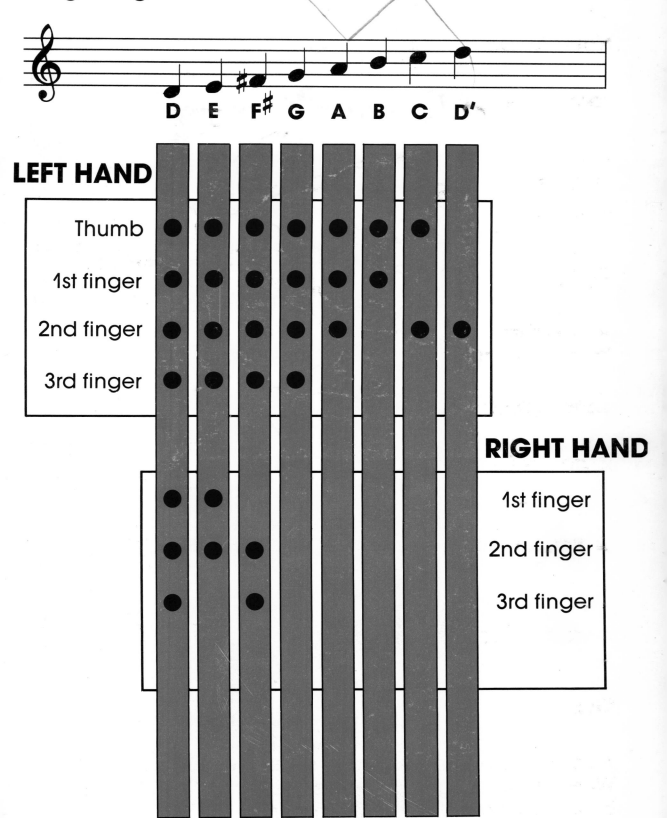